FRONT

With Blue, ch 3; join with slip st to form a ring.

Rnd 1 (Right side)**:** Ch 1, 6 sc in ring; join with slip st to first sc.

Note: Mark Rnd 1 as **right** side.

Rnd 2: Ch 1, 2 sc in same st and in each sc around; join with slip st to first sc: 12 sc.

Rnd 3: Ch 1, 2 sc in same st, sc in next sc, (2 sc in next sc, sc in next sc) around; join with slip st to first sc: 18 sc.

Rnd 4: Ch 1, 2 sc in same st, sc in next 2 sc, (2 sc in next sc, sc in next 2 sc) around; join with slip st to Front Loop Only of first sc ***(Fig. 1, page 35)***: 24 sc.

Rnd 5 (Begin ruffle)**:** Ch 3 **(counts as first dc, now and throughout)**, **turn**; working in Back Loops Only, 2 dc in same st, 3 dc in next sc and in each sc around; join with slip st to first dc: 72 dc.

Rnd 6: Ch 3, do **not** turn; working in both loops, dc in same st and in next dc, (2 dc in next dc, dc in next dc) around; join with slip st to first sc, finish off: 108 dc.

Rnd 7 (Finish ruffle)**:** With **right** side facing, join Ecru with slip st in any dc; ch 2, slip st in second ch from hook, ★ slip st in next 2 dc, ch 2, slip st in second ch from hook; repeat from ★ around to last dc, slip st in last dc; join with slip st to joining slip st, finish off.

When working the Front, it is recommended to join the yarn in different areas to keep the Front circular.

Rnd 8: With **right** side facing and working **behind** Ruffle in free loops on Rnd 4 ***(Fig. 2a, page 35)***, join Blue with sc in any sc ***(see Joining With Sc, page 34)***; sc in same st, place marker around first sc of 2-sc group just made, sc in next 3 sc, ★ 2 sc in next sc, place marker around first sc of 2-sc group just made, sc in next 3 sc; repeat from ★ around; join with slip st to first sc: 30 sc.

Rnds 9-11: Ch 1, ★ 2 sc in marked sc, remove marker and place around first sc of 2-sc group just made, sc in each sc across to next marker; repeat from ★ around; join with slip st to first sc: 48 sc.

Rnd 12: Ch 1, ★ 2 sc in marked sc, remove marker and place around first sc of 2-sc group just made, sc in each sc across to next marker; repeat from ★ around; join with slip st to Front Loop Only of first sc: 54 sc.

Rnd 13 (Begin ruffle)**:** Ch 3, **turn**; working in Back Loops Only and removing markers, 2 dc in same st, 3 dc in next sc and in each sc around; join with slip st to first dc: 162 dc.

Rnd 14: Ch 3, do **not** turn; working in both loops, dc in same st and in next dc, (2 dc in next dc, dc in next dc) around; join with slip st to first dc, finish off: 243 dc.

Rnd 15 (Finish ruffle)**:** With **right** side facing, join Green with slip st in any dc; ch 2, slip st in second ch from hook, ★ slip st in next 2 dc, ch 2, slip st in second ch from hook; repeat from ★ around; join with slip st to joining slip st, finish off.

Rnd 16: With **right** side facing and working **behind** Ruffle in free loops on Rnd 12, join Blue with sc in any sc; sc in same st, place marker around first sc of 2-sc group just made, sc in next 8 sc, ★ 2 sc in next sc, place marker around first sc of 2-sc group just made, sc in next 8 sc; repeat from ★ around; join with slip st to first sc: 60 sc.

Rnds 17-22: Repeat Rnds 9-14; at end of Rnd 22, do **not** finish off: 378 dc.

Rnd 23 (Finish ruffle)**:** Ch 2, **turn**; slip st in second ch from hook, ★ slip st in next 2 dc, ch 2, slip st in second ch from hook; repeat from ★ around to last dc, slip in last dc; join with slip st to joining slip st, finish off.

Rnd 24: With **right** side facing and working **behind** Ruffle in free loops on Rnd 20, join Blue with sc in any sc; sc in same st, place marker around first sc of 2-sc group just made, sc in next 13 sc, ★ 2 sc in next sc, place marker around first sc of 2-sc group just made, sc in next 13 sc; repeat from ★ around; join with slip st to first sc: 90 sc.

Rnds 25-30: Repeat Rnds 9-14: 513 dc.

Rnd 31: With Ecru, repeat Rnd 15.

Rnd 32: With **right** side facing and working **behind** Ruffle in free loops on Rnd 28, join Blue with sc in any sc; sc in same st, place marker around first sc of 2-sc group just made, sc in next 18 sc, ★ 2 sc in next sc, place marker around first sc of 2-sc group just made, sc in next 18 sc; repeat from ★ around; join with slip st to first sc: 120 sc.

Rnds 33-38: Repeat Rnds 9-14: 648 dc.

Rnd 39: With Green, repeat Rnd 7.

Rnd 40: With **right** side facing and working **behind** Ruffle in free loops on Rnd 36, join Blue with sc in any sc; sc in same st, place marker around first sc of 2-sc group just made, sc in next 23 sc, ★ 2 sc in next sc, place marker around first sc of 2-sc group just made, sc in next 23 sc; repeat from ★ around; join with slip st to first sc: 150 sc.

Rnds 41-46: Repeat Rnds 9-14; at end of Rnd 46, do **not** finish off: 783 dc.

Rnd 47: Repeat Rnd 23.

Rnd 48: With **right** side facing and working **behind** Ruffle in free loops on Rnd 44, join Blue with sc in any sc; sc in same st, place marker around first sc of 2-sc group just made, sc in next 28 sc, ★ 2 sc in next sc, place marker around first sc of 2-sc group just made, sc in next 28 sc; repeat from ★ around; join with slip st to first sc: 180 sc.

Rnds 49-52: Repeat Rnds 9-11 once, then repeat Rnd 9 once **more**: 204 sc.

Rnd 53: Ch 1, sc in same sc and in each sc around, removing markers; join with slip st to first sc, do **not** finish off.

JOINING

Ch 1; with **wrong** sides of Front and Back together, Front facing, and working through **both** loops on **both** layers; sc in same st and in each sc around inserting pillow form before closing; join with slip st to first sc, finish off.

freshidea

One of my passions is reading and collecting antique needlecraft books. This two-color pillow in Tunisian Simple Stitch is adapted from a needlepoint chart in a French book entitled *Encyclopedie des Ouvrages de Dames*. I could not find a copyright date on it, but an earlier owner marked it with her name and the date 1915. Since Tunisian Simple Stitches are as close to square as a stitch can get, it is a perfect medium to interpret charts from needlepoint or embroidery.

INTERMEDIATE

Finished Size:
16" (40.5 cm) square

MATERIALS

MEDIUM 4

Medium Weight Yarn
[4 ounces, 186 yards
(113 grams, 170 meters) per skein]:
- Green - 2 skeins
- Lt Green - one skein

Afghan crochet hook, size H (5 mm)
or size needed for gauge
Bobbins
Pillow form - 16" (40.5 cm) square

GAUGE: In pattern, 12 sts and
12 rows = 3$^{3}/_{4}$" (9.5 cm)

Gauge Swatch: 3$^{3}/_{4}$" (9.5 cm) square
With Green, ch 12.
Work same as Back for 12 rows.
Finish off.

BACK

With Green, ch 53.

Row 1 - Step 1: Working in Top Loops Only, insert hook in second ch from hook ***(Fig. A)***, YO and pull up a loop (2 loops on hook), pull up a loop in each ch across ***(Fig. B)*** keeping all loops on hook: 53 loops.

Fig. A

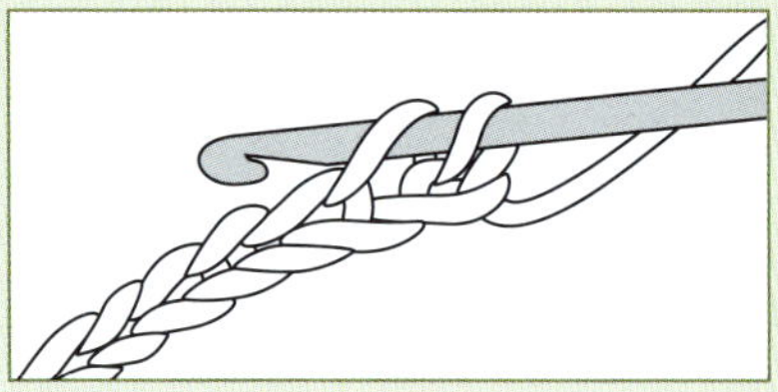

Fig. B

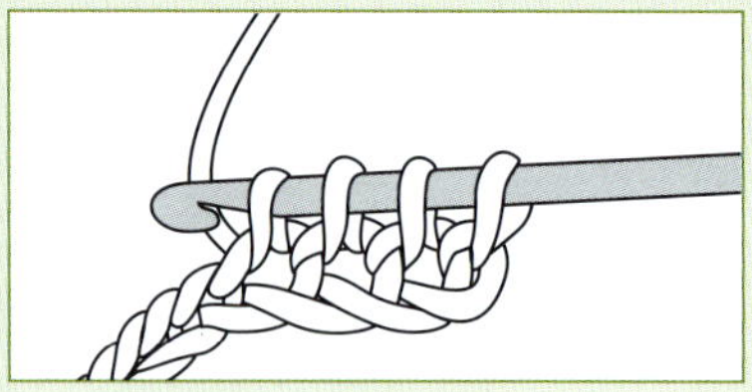

DO NOT TURN WORK - the side facing you is the **right** side.

Row 1 - Step 2: YO and draw through one loop **(Beginning Afghan St made)**, ★ YO and draw through 2 loops **(Afghan St made, *Fig. C*)**; repeat from ★ across until one loop remains on hook: 53 Afghan Sts.

Fig. C

These two steps are always counted as one row.

Instructions continued on page 8.

the perfect pillow!

There's no need to crochet an ordinary pillow, because you can create one of these stylish designs, instead! This collection of 10 patterns offers plenty of variety. Go for bold color or original texture. Try a lacy, vintage bolster or add buttons to a two-toned, contemporary look. Mary Beth Temple shares her insights and inspirations on how she created each of these designs. And with Mary Beth's instructions, you know you'll make a fun project that finishes beautifully.

Mary Beth Temple

Mary Beth Temple—"M.B." to her friends—finds that life goes better with crochet. In fact, if you've read something laugh-out-loud funny about crochet, there's a good chance Mary Beth wrote it. Her humorous essays and informative articles on yarn crafts have appeared in several popular magazines. Her talent as a designer is apparent when you see her Leisure Arts book (#4750) *DIY Afghans*. She's also the author of *Hooked for Life: Adventures of a Crochet Zealot*.

"In fact, I was writing an article about crochet," Mary Beth says, "when my friends at the Crochet Guild of America got me hooked on the idea of designing."

Mary Beth's working day is filled with designing, writing books and articles, and posting on www.alpacaaddict.blogspot.com. She also maintains a site at www.marybethtemple.com. All that seems like plenty to do, yet Mary Beth still squeezes in time to do a weekly Internet radio show about crochet called "Getting Loopy" at www.blogtalkradio.com.

Mary Beth's family time is also rich with activity. The household includes husband John, 13-year-old daughter Katie, an English Angora bunny, and a spoiled Shih Tzu who is often seen with yarn clippings stuck to her fur.

LEISURE ARTS, INC.
Little Rock, Arkansas

loop-de-loop

This pillow is densely textured from rows and rows of ruffled stitching in a lightweight yarn. Choose just a few edging colors as I did here, or go to town and tip each ruffle in a different color to really make the texture pop!

EASY +

Finished Size:
16" (40.5 cm) diameter

MATERIALS

Light Weight Yarn (LIGHT 3)
[3.5 ounces, 245 yards
(100 grams, 224 meters) per skein]:
- Blue - 5 skeins
- Green **and** Ecru - one skein **each** color

Crochet hook, size F (3.75 mm) **or** size needed for gauge
Pillow form - 16" (40.5 cm) diameter
Split-ring markers - 6

GAUGE SWATCH:
$2^1/_2$" (6.25 cm) diameter
Work through Rnd 5 of Back.

BACK

With Blue, ch 3; join with slip st to form a ring.

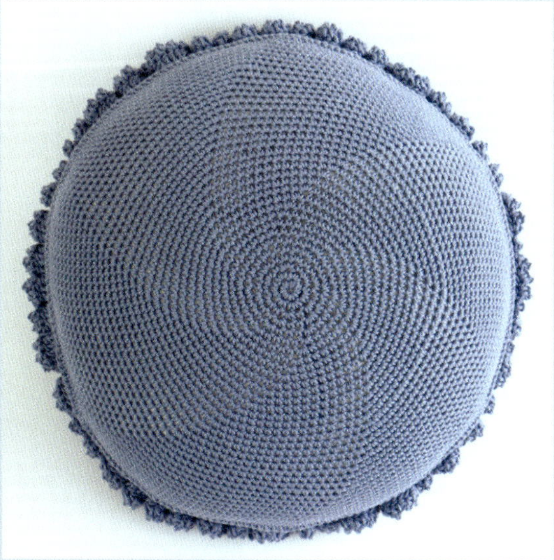

Rnd 1 (Right side)**:** Ch 1, 6 sc in ring; do **not** join, place marker to mark beginning of rnd ***(see Markers, page 34)***.

Note: Loop a short piece of yarn around any stitch to mark Rnd 1 as **right** side.

Rnd 2: 2 Sc in each sc around: 12 sc.

Rnd 3: (2 Sc in next sc, sc in next sc) around: 18 sc.

Rnd 4: ★ 2 Sc in next sc, place split-ring marker around first sc of 2-sc group just made, sc in next 2 sc; repeat from ★ around: 24 sc.

Rnds 5-34: ★ 2 Sc in marked sc, remove marker and place around first sc of 2-sc group just made, sc in each sc across to next marker; repeat from ★ around: 204 sc.

Rnd 35: Sc in each sc around; slip st in next sc; finish off.

Instructions continued on page 4.

Row 2 - Step 1: Insert hook through upright bar of second loop ***(Fig. D)***, YO and pull up loop (2 loops on hook), pull up a loop in each bar across to last bar, insert hook through last bar and the strand behind it ***(Fig. E)***, YO and pull up a loop: 53 loops.

Fig. D

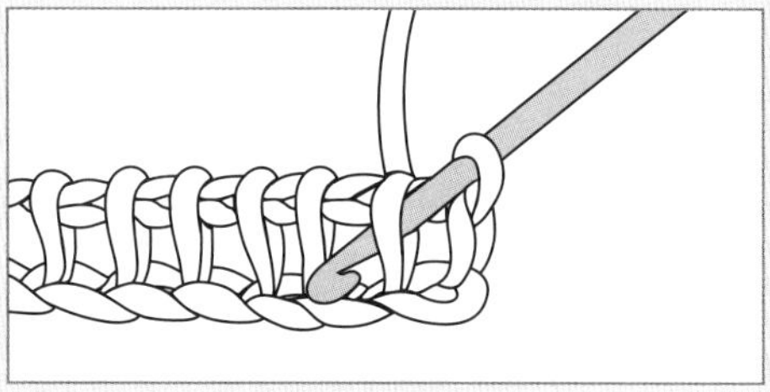

Fig. E

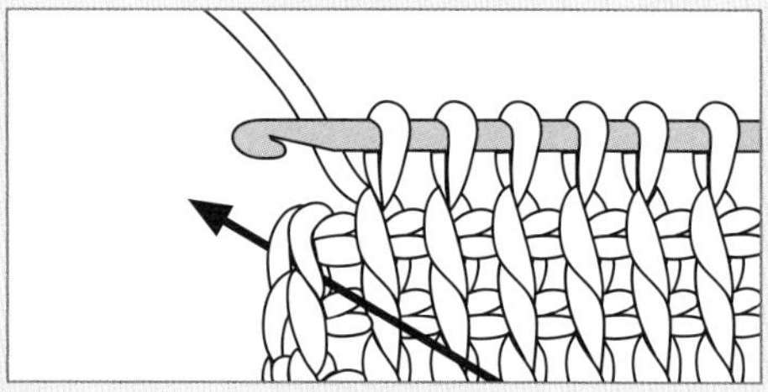

Row 2 - Step 2: Repeat Row 1 - Step 2: 53 Afghan Sts.

Rows 3-55: Repeat Row 2.

Bind-Off Row: Skip first bar, ★ insert hook through next bar, YO and draw **loosely** through bar and loop on hook **(slip stitch made)**; repeat from ★ across; finish off.

FRONT

Wind a small amount of each color onto a bobbin for each color change. When changing colors, pick up new color from under the old color to prevent holes, keep unused color on **wrong** side of work; do **not** cut yarn until color is no longer needed.

With Green, ch 53.

Row 1 - Step 1: Working in Top Loops Only, insert hook in second ch from hook, YO and pull up a loop (2 loops on hook), pull up a loop in each ch across keeping all loops on hook: 53 loops.

Row 1 - Step 2: YO and draw through one loop, ★ YO and draw through 2 loops; repeat from ★ across until one loop remains on hook: 53 Afghan Sts.

Row 2 - Step 1: Insert hook through upright bar of second loop, YO and pull up loop (2 loops on hook), pull up a loop in each bar across to last bar, insert hook through last bar and the strand behind it, YO and pull up a loop: 53 loops.

Row 2 - Step 2: Repeat Row 1 - Step 2: 53 Afghan Sts.

Row 3: Repeat Row 2.

You may find that changing colors causes your gauge to tighten. Do **not** hesitate to change to a larger size hook to keep your gauge consistent.

Row 4 - Step 1: With Green pull up a loop in next 4 bars (5 loops on hook), drop Green to the back, with Lt Green and leaving a long end to be worked in later, pull up a loop in next bar ***(Fig. F)***, pull up a loop in next bar, drop Lt Green to the back, with Green pull up a loop in next 5 bars, with Lt Green pull up a loop in next 4 bars, (with Green pull up a loop in next bar, with Lt Green pull up a loop in next 2 bars) 3 times, with Green pull up a loop in next 6 bars, with Lt Green pull up a loop in next 3 bars, with Green pull up a loop in next 2 bars, with Lt Green pull up a loop in next 5 bars, with Green pull up a loop in next 3 bars, with Lt Green pull up a loop in next 6 bars, with Green pull up a loop in last 4 bars: 53 loops.

Fig. F

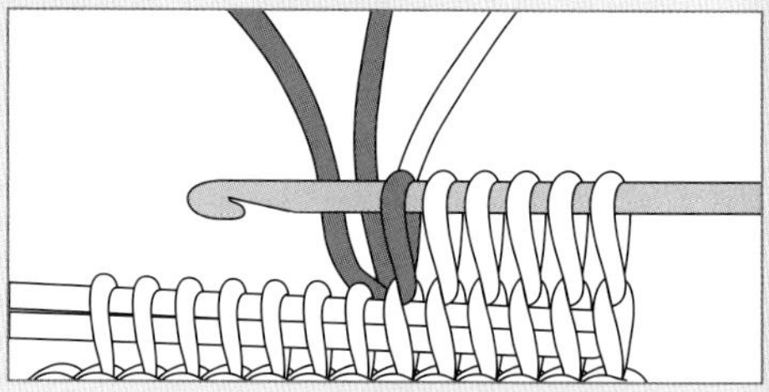

Row 4 - Step 2: Completing Step 2 in same manner, draw loop through using the color of the second loop on the hook ***(Fig. G)***: 53 Afghan Sts.

Fig. G

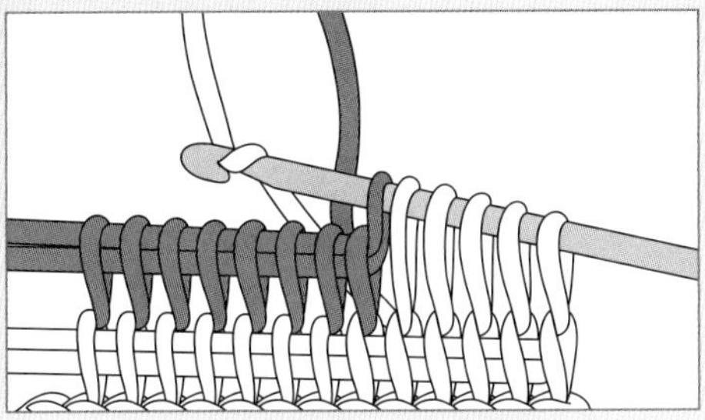

Rows 5-55: Continue in same manner, working from **right** to **left** across for Step 1 and **left** to **right** back across for Step 2 on each row of chart.

Bind-Off Row: Skip first bar, ★ insert hook through next bar, YO and draw yarn **loosely** through bar and loop on hook; repeat from ★ across; do **not** finish off.

EDGING

Rnd 1 (Joining rnd)**:** Ch 1; with **wrong** sides of Front and Back together, Front facing and working through **both** layers, sc evenly around working ch-2 at each corner and inserting pillow form before closing; join with slip st to first sc.

Rnd 2: Ch 3 **(counts as first dc)**, ★ dc in next sc and in each sc across to next corner ch-2 sp, 3 dc in corner ch-2 sp; repeat from ★ around; join with slip st to first dc.

Rnd 3: Ch 1, sc in same st and in each dc around working 3 sc in center dc of each corner 3-dc group; join with slip st to first sc, finish off.

KEY
□ - Green
■ - Lt Green

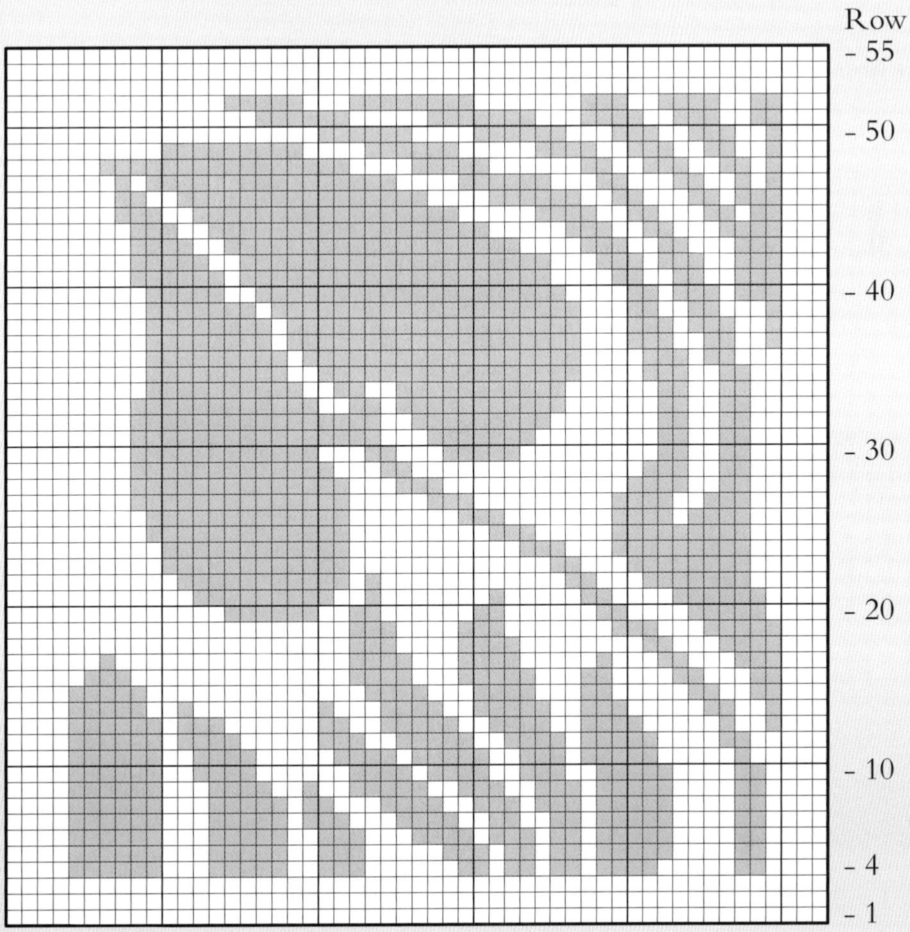

artdeco

I really wanted to experiment with these unusually shaped motifs, but didn't want to spend hours assembling them—I would always rather crochet than sew seams. So this pillow is constructed with the brighter colors as motifs, but the dark brown is worked in rows across the width of the pillow, which cuts way down on the seaming time.

INTERMEDIATE

Finished Size:
12"h x 22"w (30.5 cm x 56 cm)

MATERIALS

LIGHT 3

Light Weight Yarn
[2.5 ounces, 168 yards
(70 grams, 154 meters) per skein]:
Brown - 2 skeins
Orange **and** Green - one skein each color
Crochet hook, size G (4 mm) **or** size needed for gauge
Pillow form - 12"h x 22"w (30.5 cm x 56 cm)
Yarn needle

GAUGE: Each Full Motif = 2" (5 cm) across widest part
14 dc = 4" (10 cm)

Gauge Swatch: 2" (5 cm)
Work same as Full Motif.

FRONT

FULL MOTIF (Make 38)

With Orange, ch 4; join with slip st to form a ring.

Rnd 1 (Right side)**:** Ch 3 **(counts as first dc, now and throughout),** 11 dc in ring; join with slip st to first dc, finish off: 12 dc.

Note: Loop a short piece of yarn around any stitch to mark Rnd 1 as **right** side.

Rnd 2: With **right** side facing, join Green with dc in same st as joining ***(see Joining With Dc, page 34)***; dc in same st, 2 dc in each of next 5 dc, (hdc, sc) in next dc, 2 sc in next dc, (hdc, dc) in next dc, (dc, hdc) in next dc, 2 sc in next dc, (sc, hdc) in last dc; join with slip st to first dc, finish off: 24 sts.

TOP HALF MOTIF

(Make 6)

With Orange, ch 4; join with slip st to form a ring.

Row 1 (Right side)**:** Ch 3, 5 dc in ring; finish off: 6 dc.

Note: Mark Row 1 as **right** side.

Row 2: With **right** side facing, join Green with hdc in first dc ***(see Joining With Hdc, page 34)***; sc in same st, 2 sc in next dc, (hdc, dc) in next dc, (dc, hdc) in next dc, 2 sc in next dc, (sc, hdc) in last dc; finish off: 12 sts.

Instructions continued on page 12.

BOTTOM HALF MOTIF

(Make 6)
With Orange, ch 4; join with slip st to form a ring.

Row 1 (Right side)**:** Ch 3, 5 dc in ring; finish off: 6 dc.

Note: Mark Row 1 as **right** side.

Row 2: With **right** side facing, join Green with dc in first dc; dc in same st, 2 dc in each of last 5 dc; finish off: 12 dc.

RIGHT SIDE HALF MOTIF (Make 4)

With Orange, ch 4; join with slip st to form a ring.

Row 1 (Right side)**:** Ch 3, 5 dc in ring; finish off: 6 dc.

Note: Mark Row 1 as **right** side.

Row 2: With **right** side facing, join Green with dc in first dc; dc in same st, 2 dc in each of next 2 dc, (hdc, sc) in next dc, 2 sc in next dc, (hdc, dc) in last dc; finish off: 12 sts.

LEFT SIDE HALF MOTIF

(Make 4)
With Orange, ch 4; join with slip st to form a ring.

Row 1 (Right side)**:** Ch 3, 5 dc in ring; finish off: 6 dc.

Note: Mark Row 1 as **right** side.

Row 2: With **right** side facing, join Green with dc in first dc; hdc in same st, 2 sc in next dc, (sc, hdc) in next dc, 2 dc in each of last 3 dc; finish off: 12 sts.

ASSEMBLY

FIRST STRIP

With **right** side of one Bottom Half Motif facing, join Brown with dc in first dc; ★ † (2 dc in next dc, dc in next dc) twice, 2 dc in each of next 2 dc, dc in next dc, (2 dc in next dc, dc in next dc) twice †; with **right** side of **next Bottom Half Motif** facing, dc in first dc; repeat from ★ 4 times **more**, then repeat from † to † once; finish off.

SECOND STRIP

With **right** side of one Right Side Half Motif facing, join Brown with dc in first dc; 2 dc in next dc, (dc in next dc, 2 dc in next dc) twice, holding **First Strip** with **right** side facing, skip first 9 dc on **first Bottom Half Motif**, slip st in sp **before** next dc ***(Fig. A)***; ★ with **right** side of **next Full Motif** facing, dc in same st as joining, (2 dc in next dc, dc in next dc) twice, 2 dc in each of next 2 dc, dc in next dc, (2 dc in next dc, dc in next dc) twice, skip first 9 dc on **next Bottom Half Motif**, slip st in sp **before** next dc; repeat from ★ 4 times **more**; with **right** side of one Left Side Half Motif facing, skip first 6 sts, (2 dc in next dc, dc in next dc) across; finish off.

Fig. A

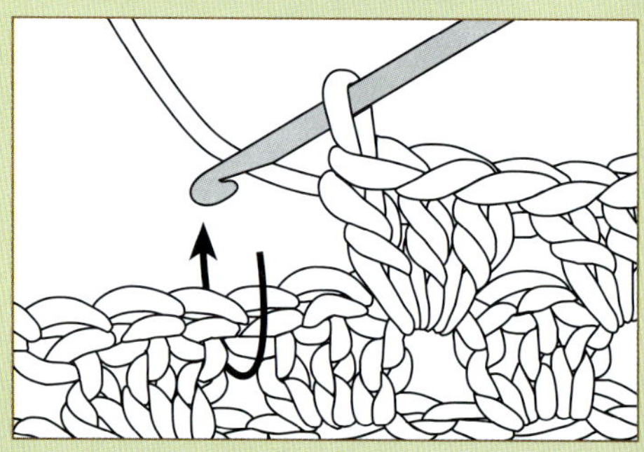

THIRD STRIP

With **right** side of one Full Motif facing, join Brown with dc in same st as joining; ★ † (2 dc in next dc, dc in next dc) twice, 2 dc in each of next 2 dc, dc in next dc, (2 dc in next dc, dc in next dc) twice †, holding **previous Strip** with **right** side facing, skip first 9 dc on **Full Motif**, slip st in sp **before** next dc, with **right** side of **next Full Motif** facing, dc in same st as joining; repeat from ★ 4 times **more**, then repeat from † to † once; finish off.

FOURTH STRIP

With **right** side of one Right Side Half Motif facing, join Brown with dc in first dc; 2 dc in next dc, (dc in next dc, 2 dc in next dc) twice, holding **previous Strip** with **right** side facing, skip first 9 dc on **first Full Motif**, slip st in sp **before** next dc; ★ with **right** side of **next Full Motif** facing, dc in same st as joining, (2 dc in next dc, dc in next dc) twice, 2 dc in each of next 2 dc, dc in next dc, (2 dc in next dc, dc in next dc) twice, skip first 9 dc on **next Full Motif**, slip st in sp **before** next dc; repeat from ★ 4 times **more**; with **right** side of one Left Side Half Motif facing, skip first 6 sts, (2 dc in next dc, dc in next dc) across; finish off.

FIFTH THROUGH EIGHTH STRIPS

Repeat Third and Fourth Strips twice.

Using Brown and with **right** sides together, working through **outside** loops, whipstitch Strips together; then whipstitch Top Half Motifs along top edge of Eighth Strip in same manner.

BORDER

With **right** side facing and working in end of rows and in beginning ring on Side and Half Motifs, join Brown with sc in first top corner ***(see Joining With Sc, page 34)***; work 74 sc evenly spaced across Top Half Motifs, ch 1; work 45 sc evenly spaced across Side Motifs, ch 1; work 75 sc evenly spaced across Bottom Half Motifs, ch 1; work 45 sc evenly spaced across Side Motifs, ch 1; join with slip st to first sc, finish off: 240 sc and 4 ch-1 sps.

BACK

BODY

With Brown, ch 77.

Row 1 (Right side)**:** Dc in fourth ch from hook **(3 skipped chs count as first dc)** and in each ch across: 75 dc.

Note: Mark Row 1 as **right** side.

Row 2: Ch 3, turn; dc in next dc and in each dc across.

Repeat Row 2 until piece measures 12" (30.5 cm) from beginning ch; finish off.

BORDER

With **right** side facing, join Brown with sc in first top corner; sc in each st across, ch 1; work 45 sc evenly spaced across end of rows, ch 1; working in free loops of beginning ch ***(Fig. 2b, page 35)***, sc in each st across, ch 1; work 45 sc evenly spaced across end of rows, ch 1; join with slip st to first sc, finish off: 240 sc and 4 ch-1 sps.

EDGING

Rnd 1 (Joining rnd)**:** With **right** sides of Front and Back together, Front facing, and working through **both** layers, join Brown with sc in any corner ch-1 sp; ch 1, sc in same sp, ★ sc in each sc across to next corner ch-1 sp, (sc, ch 1, sc) in corner ch-1 sp; repeat from ★ 2 times **more**, insert pillow form, sc in each sc across; join with slip st to first sc: 248 sc and 4 ch-1 sps.

Rnd 2: (Slip st, ch 3, 6 dc) in next ch-1 sp, ★ skip next 2 sc, sc in next sc, (skip next 2 sc, 7 dc in next sc, skip next 2 sc, sc in next sc) across to within 2 sc of next corner ch-1 sp, skip next 2 sc, 7 dc in corner ch-1 sp; repeat from ★ 2 times **more**, skip next 2 sc, sc in next sc, skip next 2 sc, (7 dc in next sc, skip next 2 sc, sc in next sc, skip next 2 sc) across; join with slip st to first dc, finish off.

buttonedup

This simple, textured pillow is the perfect background for any elegant buttons you choose, and would look terrific in a den, study, or library.

EASY +

Finished Size:
16"h x 20"w (40.5 cm x 51 cm)

MATERIALS

MEDIUM 4

Medium Weight Yarn
[4 ounces, 186 yards
(113 grams, 170 meters) per skein]:
Green - 2 skeins
Ecru - one skein
Crochet hook, size I (5.5 mm) **or** size needed for gauge
Pillow form - 16"h x 20"w (40.5 cm x 51 cm)
1$^{3}/_{16}$" (30 mm) Buttons - 5
$^{7}/_{8}$" (22 mm) Buttons - 5
Tapestry needle

GAUGE: In pattern, 5 3-sc groups and 13 rows = 3$^{3}/_{4}$" (9.5 cm)

Gauge Swatch: 3$^{3}/_{4}$" (9.5 cm) square
With Green, ch 15.
Row 1: 3 Sc in third ch from hook, (skip next 2 chs, 3 sc in next ch) across: 5 3-sc groups.
Rows 2-13: Ch 1, turn; skip first sc, 3 sc in next sc, (skip next 2 sc, 3 sc in next sc) across to last sc, leave last sc unworked.
Finish off.

BODY (Make 2)

With Ecru ch 27, drop Ecru, with Green ch 54: 81 chs.

Row 1 (Right side)**:** 3 Sc in third ch from hook, (skip next 2 chs, 3 sc in next ch) 17 times changing to Ecru in last sc made ***(Fig. 3a, page 35)***, (skip next 2 chs, 3 sc in next ch) across: 27 3-sc groups (18 Green and 9 Ecru).

Note: Loop a short piece of yarn around any stitch on Row 1 to mark **right** side.

Row 2: Ch 1, turn; skip first sc, 3 sc in next sc, (skip next 2 sc, 3 sc in next sc) 8 times changing to Green in last sc made, (skip next 2 sc, 3 sc in next sc) across to last sc, leave last sc unworked.

Row 3: Ch 1 turn; skip first sc, 3 sc in next sc, (skip next 2 sc, 3 sc in next sc) 17 times changing to Ecru in last sc made, (skip next 2 sc, 3 sc in next sc) across to last sc, leave last sc unworked.

Repeat Rows 2 and 3 for pattern until piece measures approximately 16" (40.5 cm) from beginning ch, ending by working Row 3; finish off Ecru and cut Green.

ACCENT LINE

With **right** side of Body facing and working in sts along color change, insert hook in first st at beginning ch from **front** to **back**, holding Green on **wrong** side, YO and pull up a loop, ★ insert hook in st on next row, YO and draw through st and loop on hook; repeat from ★ across; finish off.

FINISHING

Stack one smaller button on top of one larger button, lining up holes. Using photo as a guide for placement, sew stacked button to Accent Line using 3 strands of Green. Tie strands in a knot; cut ends and fray.

Repeat with remaining buttons, this will be the front.

EDGING

Rnd 1 (Joining rnd)**:** With **wrong** sides of Body pieces together, matching colors and front facing, join Ecru with sc in first st on Ecru section ***(see Joining With Sc, page 34)*** working through **both** layers; sc in each st across to next corner, 3 sc in corner; working in end of rows, sc evenly across to next corner, 3 sc in corner, sc in each st across to color change changing to Green in last sc made, sc in each sc across to next corner, 3 sc in corner, insert pillow form; working in end of rows, sc evenly across to next corner, 3 sc in corner; sc in each st across; join with slip st to first sc.

Rnd 2: Ch 1, working from **left** to **right**, work reverse sc in same st ***(Figs. 4a-d, page 35)*** and in each sc around to color change changing to Ecru in last sc made, cut Green; work reverse sc in next sc and in each sc around; join with slip st to first st, finish off.

alfresco

I wanted to create a pillow with some open spaces between crochet stitches so that I could play with additional color and pattern on the background fabric. Choose a stack of coordinating colors, or use up scraps for the circles section.

EASY +

Finished Size:
18" (45.5 cm) square

MATERIALS

MEDIUM 4

- Medium Weight Yarn [3.5 ounces, 213 yards (100 grams, 195 meters) per skein]:
  - MC (Blue) - 2 skeins
  - Green, Teal, Lt Blue, Dk Blue, and Purple - one skein **each** color
- Crochet hook, size G (4 mm) **or** size needed for gauge
- Pillow form - 18" (45.5 cm) square covered with fabric as desired
- Yarn needle

GAUGE: Each Circle = 2" (5 cm) diameter
In pattern, (sc, ch 2, sc) 6 times = 4" (10 cm)

Gauge Swatch: 2" (5 cm)
Work same as Circle.

FRONT

CIRCLE PANEL

CIRCLE (Make 24)

With desired color, ch 4; join with slip st to form a ring.

Rnd 1 (Right side)**:** Ch 3 **(counts as first dc)**, 11 dc in ring; join with slip st to first dc: 12 dc.

Note: Loop a short piece of yarn around any stitch to mark Rnd 1 as **right** side.

Rnd 2: Ch 1, 2 sc in same st and in each dc around; join with slip st to first sc, finish off: 24 sc.

Sew Circles together randomly, sewing through Back Loop Only ***(Fig. 1, page 35)*** of one sc on each Circle to form a Panel of 3 Circles wide x 8 Circles long.

BODY

With MC, ch 57.

Row 1 (Right side)**:** Sc in second ch from hook, skip next ch, (sc, ch 2, sc) in next ch, ★ skip next 2 chs, (sc, ch 2, sc) in next ch; repeat from ★ across to last 2 chs, skip next ch, sc in last ch: 18 ch-2 sps.

Note: Mark Row 1 as **right** side.

Row 2: Ch 1, turn; sc in first sc, (sc, ch 2, sc) in next ch-2 sp and in each ch-2 sp across to last 2 sc, skip next sc, sc in last sc.

Repeat Row 2 for pattern until piece measures 18" (45.5 cm) from beginning ch, ending by working a **right** side row.

Trim: Ch 1, do **not** turn; work 56 sc evenly spaced across end of rows; finish off.

Using photo as a guide for placement, sew Circle Panel to Body Trim, sewing through Back Loop Only of one stitch on both pieces.

BACK

With MC, ch 84.

Row 1 (Right side)**:** Sc in second ch from hook, skip next ch, (sc, ch 2, sc) in next ch, ★ skip next 2 chs, (sc, ch 2, sc) in next ch; repeat from ★ across to last 2 chs, skip next ch, sc in last ch: 27 ch-2 sps.

Note: Mark Row 1 as **right** side.

Row 2: Ch 1, turn; sc in first sc, (sc, ch 2, sc) in next ch-2 sp and in each ch-2 sp across to last 2 sc, skip next sc, sc in last sc.

Repeat Row 2 for pattern until piece measures 18" (45.5 cm) from beginning ch, ending by working a **right** side row; finish off.

JOINING

With **wrong** sides of Front and Back together, Front facing, matching sts and working through **both** layers and in end of rows, join MC with sc in first row ***(see Joining With Sc, page 34)***; work 55 sc evenly spaced across, ch 1; working across last row, work 36 sc evenly spaced across to Trim, working in sts on Back and in one sc on each of next 3 Circles, work 20 sc evenly spaced across, ch 1; working in end of rows on Back and in one sc on each of next 8 Circles, work 56 sc evenly spaced across, ch 1, working in free loops of beginning ch on Back ***(Fig. 2b, page 35)*** and in one sc on each of next 3 Circles, work 20 sc evenly spaced across to Trim, insert pillow form, work 36 sc evenly spaced across, ch 1; join with slip st to first sc, finish off.

happypatches

There is something about patchwork quilts that always makes me want to reinterpret their many shapes in crochet! This quick color-work pillow would look great in a country or rustic décor.

EASY +

Finished Size:
16" (40.5 cm) square

MATERIALS

Medium Weight Yarn (MEDIUM 4)
[5 ounces, 256 yards
(140 grams, 234 meters) per skein]:
- Blue - 2 skeins
- Black and Rose - one skein **each** color

Crochet hook, size H (5 mm) **or** size needed for gauge
Bobbins
Pillow form - 16" (40.5 cm) square

GAUGE: 12 dc and 7 rows = 3½" (9 cm)

Gauge Swatch: 3½" (9 cm) square
With Blue, ch 14.
Row 1: Dc in fourth ch from hook **(3 skipped chs count as first dc)** and in each ch across: 12 dc.
Rows 2-7: Ch 3 **(counts as first dc)**, turn; dc in next dc and in each dc across.
Finish off.

FRONT

Wind a small amount of each color onto a bobbin for each color change. When changing colors, pick up new color from under the old color to prevent holes, keep unused color on **wrong** side of work; do **not** cut yarn until color is no longer needed.

With Blue, ch 60.

Row 1 (Right side)**:** Dc in fourth ch from hook **(3 skipped chs count as first dc, now and throughout)** and in each ch across: 58 dc.

Note: Loop a short piece of yarn around any stitch to mark Row 1 as **right** side.

Rows 2-5: Ch 3 **(counts as first dc, now and throughout)**, turn; dc in next dc and in each dc across.

Row 6: Ch 3, turn; dc in next 7 dc changing to Rose in last dc made ***(Fig. 3b, page 35)***, dc in next 14 dc changing to Blue in last dc made, dc in next dc changing to Black, dc in next 14 dc changing to Rose in last dc made, dc in next 13 dc changing to Blue in last dc made, dc in last 8 dc.

Continue to change colors in same manner throughout.

Row 7: Ch 3, turn; dc in next 7 dc, with Rose dc in next 11 dc, with Black dc in next 14 dc, with Blue dc in next 3 dc, with Black dc in next dc, with Rose dc in next 13 dc, with Blue dc in last 8 dc.

Instructions continued on page 20.

Row 8: Ch 3, turn; dc in next 7 dc, with Rose dc in next 11 dc, with Black dc in next 3 dc, with Blue dc in next 5 dc, with Black dc in next 14 dc, with Rose dc in next 9 dc, with Blue dc in last 8 dc.

Row 9: Ch 3, turn; dc in next 7 dc, with Rose dc in next 7 dc, with Black dc in next 14 dc, with Blue dc in next 7 dc, with Black dc in next 5 dc, with Rose dc in next 9 dc, with Blue dc in last 8 dc.

Row 10: Ch 3, turn; dc in next 7 dc, with Rose dc in next 7 dc, with Black dc in next 7 dc, with Blue dc in next 9 dc, with Black dc in next 14 dc, with Rose dc in next 5 dc, with Blue dc in last 8 dc.

Row 11: Ch 3, turn; dc in next 7 dc, with Rose dc in next 3 dc, with Black dc in next 14 dc, with Blue dc in next 11 dc, with Black dc in next 9 dc, with Rose dc in next 5 dc, with Blue dc in last 8 dc.

Row 12: Ch 3, turn; dc in next 7 dc, with Rose dc in next 3 dc, with Black dc in next 11 dc, with Blue dc in next 13 dc, with Black dc in next 14 dc, with Rose dc in next dc, with Blue dc in last 8 dc.

Row 13: Ch 3, turn; dc in next 7 dc, with Black dc in next 14 dc, with Blue dc in next 14 dc, with Black dc in next 13 dc, with Rose dc in next dc, with Blue dc in last 8 dc.

Row 14: Ch 3, turn; dc in next 7 dc, with Black dc in next 28 dc, with Blue dc in next dc and in each dc across.

Row 15: Ch 3, turn; dc in next 7 dc, with Black dc in next dc, with Blue dc in next 13 dc, with Black dc in next 14 dc, with Blue dc in next dc, with Black dc in next 13 dc, with Blue dc in last 8 dc.

Row 16: Ch 3, turn; dc in next 7 dc, with Black dc in next 11 dc, with Blue dc in next 3 dc, with Black dc in next 14 dc, with Blue dc in next 11 dc, with Black dc in next 3 dc, with Blue dc in last 8 dc.

Row 17: Ch 3, turn; dc in next 7 dc, with Black dc in next 5 dc, with Blue dc in next 9 dc, with Black dc in next 14 dc, with Blue dc in next 5 dc, with Black dc in next 9 dc, with Blue dc in last 8 dc.

Row 18: Ch 3, turn; dc in next 7 dc, with Black dc in next 7 dc, with Blue dc in next 7 dc, with Black dc in next 14 dc, with Blue dc in next 7 dc, with Black dc in next 7 dc, with Blue dc in last 8 dc.

Row 19: Ch 3, turn; dc in next 7 dc, with Black dc in next 9 dc, with Blue dc in next 5 dc, with Black dc in next 14 dc, with Blue dc in next 9 dc, with Black dc in next 5 dc, with Blue dc in last 8 dc.

Row 20: Ch 3, turn; dc in next 7 dc, with Black dc in next 3 dc, with Blue dc in next 11 dc, with Black dc in next 14 dc, with Blue dc in next 3 dc, with Black dc in next 11 dc, with Blue dc in last 8 dc.

Row 21: Ch 3, turn; dc in next 7 dc, with Black dc in next 13 dc, with Blue dc in next dc, with Black dc in next 14 dc, with Blue dc in next 13 dc, with Black dc in next dc, with Blue dc in last 8 dc.

Row 22: Ch 3, turn; dc in next 7 dc, with Rose dc in next dc, with Black dc in next 14 dc, with Blue dc in next 13 dc, with Black dc in next 14 dc, with Blue dc in last 8 dc.

Row 23: Ch 3, turn; dc in next 7 dc, with Rose dc in next dc, with Black dc in next 13 dc, with Blue dc in next 11 dc, with Black dc in next 14 dc, with Rose dc in next 3 dc, with Blue dc in last 8 dc.

Row 24: Ch 3, turn; dc in next 7 dc, with Rose dc in next 5 dc, with Black dc in next 14 dc, with Blue dc in next 9 dc, with Black dc in next 11 dc, with Rose dc in next 3 dc, with Blue dc in last 8 dc.

Row 25: Ch 3, turn; dc in next 7 dc, with Rose dc in next 5 dc, with Black dc in next 9 dc, with Blue dc in next 7 dc, with Black dc in next 14 dc, with Rose dc in next 7 dc, with Blue dc in last 8 dc.

Row 26: Ch 3, turn; dc in next 7 dc, with Rose dc in next 9 dc, with Black dc in next 14 dc, with Blue dc in next 5 dc, with Black dc in next 7 dc, with Rose dc in next 7 dc, with Blue dc in last 8 dc.

Row 27: Ch 3, turn; dc in next 7 dc, with Rose dc in next 9 dc, with Black dc in next 5 dc, with Blue dc in next 3 dc, with Black dc in next 14 dc, with Rose dc in next 11 dc, with Blue dc in last 8 dc.

Row 28: Ch 3, turn; dc in next 7 dc, with Rose dc in next 13 dc, with Black dc in next 14 dc, with Blue dc in next dc, with Black dc in next 3 dc, with Rose dc in next 11 dc, with Blue dc in last 8 dc.

Row 29: Ch 3, turn; dc in next 7 dc, with Rose dc in next 13 dc, with Black dc in next 15 dc, with Rose dc in next 14 dc, with Blue dc in last 8 dc.

Cut Black and Rose.

Rows 30-34: Ch 3, turn; dc in next dc and in each dc across.

Finish off.

BACK

With Blue, ch 60.

Row 1 (Right side)**:** Dc in fourth ch from hook and in each ch across: 58 dc.

Note: Mark Row 1 as **right** side.

Rows 2-34: Ch 3, turn; dc in next dc and in each dc across.

Finish off.

JOINING

With **wrong** sides of Front and Back together, Front facing, and working through **both** layers, join Blue with sc in first dc on Row 34 ***(see Joining With Sc, page 34)***; sc evenly around working ch 1 at each corner and inserting pillow form before closing; join with slip st to first sc, finish off.

tempting texture

A little texture, a little sparkle, and very simple stitching make this over-sized pillow a terrific fashion statement for any room in the house! It is perfect for the floor or on a bed or chair, and will be the perfect companion for everything from homework to chatting to movie-watching!

EASY

Finished Size:
20" (51 cm) square

MATERIALS

Medium Weight Yarn (MEDIUM 4)
[3.5 ounces, 205 yards
(100 grams, 187 meters) per skein]:
Blue - 4 skeins
[1.75 ounces, 115 yards
(50 grams, 105 meters) per skein]:
Silver - 3 skeins
Crochet hook, size H (5 mm) **or** size needed for gauge
Pillow form - 20" (51 cm) square

GAUGE: In Back pattern,
14 dc and 7 rows = 4" (10 cm)

Gauge Swatch: 4" (10 cm) square
With Blue, ch 16.
Row 1: Dc in fourth ch from hook **(3 skipped chs count as first dc)** and in each ch across: 14 dc.
Rows 2-7: Ch 3 **(counts as first dc)**, turn; dc in next dc and in each dc across.
Finish off.

STITCH GUIDE

DECREASE (uses next 3 dc)
Pull up a loop in each of next 3 dc, YO and draw through all 4 loops on hook **(counts as one sc)**.

FRONT

With Silver, ch 69.

Row 1 (Right side)**:** Sc in second ch from hook and in each ch across: 68 sc.

Note: Loop a short piece of yarn around any stitch to mark Row 1 as **right** side and bottom edge.

Row 2: Ch 1, turn; sc in each sc across changing to Blue in last sc made ***(Fig. 3a, page 35)***; cut Silver.

Row 3: Ch 3 **(counts as first dc, now and throughout)**, turn; 2 dc in same st, 3 dc in next sc and in each sc across: 204 dc.

Rows 4 and 5: Ch 3, turn; dc in next dc and in each dc across.

Row 6: Ch 1, turn; pull up a loop in each of first 3 dc, YO and draw through all 4 loops on hook **(counts as first sc)**, decrease across changing to Silver in last sc made; do **not** cut Blue, carry loosely along edge: 68 sc.

Row 7: Ch 1, turn; sc in each sc across.

Row 8: Ch 1, turn; sc in each sc across changing to Blue in last sc made; cut Silver.

Rows 9-62: Repeat Rows 3-8, 9 times; at end of Row 62, do **not** change colors.

Finish off.

BACK

With Blue, ch 70.

Row 1 (Right side)**:** Dc in fourth ch from hook **(3 skipped chs count as first dc)** and in each ch across: 68 dc.

Note: Mark Row 1 as **right** side.

Rows 2-35: Ch 3, turn; dc in next dc and in each dc across.

Finish off.

JOINING

With **wrong** sides and bottom edges of Front and Back together, Front facing and working through **both** layers, join Silver with sc in first top corner ***(see Joining With Sc, page 34)***; sc in each st across, † ch 1; work 68 sc evenly spaced across end of rows, (ch 1, **turn**; sc in each sc across) twice, ch 1, slip st in end of next row †; working in free loops of beginning ch ***(Fig. 2b, page 35)***, sc in each ch across, insert pillow form, repeat from † to † once; join with slip st to first sc, finish off.

all-a-whirl

This fun-to-make pillow can be made in any weight or color of yarn—pick your yarn and an appropriate hook, and stitch from the center out until the top is as large as you want it to be!

EASY

Finished Size:
16" (40.5 cm) diameter

MATERIALS

MEDIUM 4

- Medium Weight Yarn [3 ounces, 185 yards (85 grams, 170 meters) per skein]: 2 skeins
- Crochet hook, size H (5 mm) **or** size needed for gauge
- Pillow form - 16" (40.5 cm) diameter covered with fabric as desired

GAUGE SWATCH:
$1^{3}/_{4}$" (4.5 cm) diameter
Work through Rnd 3 of Body.

BODY (Make 2)

Ch 4; join with slip st to form a ring.

Rnd 1 (Right side)**:** Ch 1, 7 sc in ring; join with slip st in first sc.

Note: Loop a short piece of yarn around any stitch to mark Rnd 1 as **right** side.

Rnd 2: Ch 1, 2 sc in same st and in each sc around; join with slip st to first sc: 14 sc.

Rnd 3: Ch 1, sc in same st, 2 sc in next sc, (sc in next sc, 2 sc in next sc) around; join with slip st to first sc: 21 sc.

Rnd 4: Ch 4, ★ skip next 3 sc, sc in next sc, ch 4; repeat from ★ 4 times **more**, sc in same st as joining slip st, place marker around sc just made to mark beginning of rnd: 6 sc and 6 ch-4 sps.

Rnd 5: ★ Ch 4, 2 sc in next ch-4 sp, sc in next sc; repeat from ★ 5 times **more**: 18 sc and 6 ch-4 sps.

Rnd 6: ★ Ch 4, 2 sc in next ch-4 sp, sc in next 2 sc, skip next sc; repeat from ★ 5 times **more**: 24 sc and 6 ch-4 sps.

Rnd 7: ★ Ch 4, 2 sc in next ch-4 sp, sc in next 3 sc, skip next sc; repeat from ★ 5 times **more**: 30 sc and 6 ch-4 sps.

Rnds 8-29: ★ Ch 4, 2 sc in next ch-4 sp, sc in each sc across to last sc of section, skip last sc; repeat from ★ 5 times **more**: 162 sc and 6 ch-4 sps.

Rnd 30: ★ Ch 4, 2 sc in next ch-4 sp, sc in each sc across to last sc of section, skip last sc; repeat from ★ 5 times **more**, slip st in first ch-4 sp, finish off: 168 sc and 6 ch-4 sps.

EDGING

Rnd 1 (Joining rnd)**:** With **wrong** sides of both Body pieces together and working through **both** loops on **both** layers, join yarn with sc in firstsc of any section ***(see Joining With Sc, page 34)***; sc in each sc across section, 4 sc in next ch-4 sp, (sc in each sc across next section, 3 sc in next ch-4 sp) twice, sc in each sc across next section, 4 sc in next ch-4 sp, insert pillow form, (sc in each sc across next section, 3 sc in next ch-4 sp) twice; join with slip st to first sc: 188 sc.

Rnd 2: Ch 1, sc in same st, ch 6, skip next 3 sc, ★ sc in next sc, ch 6, skip next 3 sc; repeat from ★ around; join with slip st to first sc: 47 ch-6 sps.

Rnd 3: Slip st in next ch-6 sp, ch 1, (3 sc, hdc, 2 dc, hdc, 3 sc) in same sp and in each ch-6 sp around; join with slip st to first sc, finish off.

a little luxury

While I am happy to live in the modern world, I love the look of lacy Victorian textiles. This white neck roll drips with lace—change up the lining color to coordinate with your existing color scheme.

INTERMEDIATE

Finished Size:
6" diameter x 20" long (15 cm x 51 cm) (excluding End Edgings)

MATERIALS

LACE 0

- Bedspread Weight Thread (size 10) [282 yards (258 meters) per ball]:
  2 balls
- Steel crochet hook, size 6 (1.8 mm) **or** size needed for gauge
- Pillow form - 6" diameter x 20" long (15 cm x 51 cm) covered with fabric as desired
- Assorted Ribbon (the photo model has a wide sheer, solid, and lace)

GAUGE: 13 sc = 2" (5 cm)

Gauge Swatch: $3^1/_2$" x $2^1/_2$" (9 cm x 6.25 cm)
Ch 22.
Work same as Body for 8 rows.
Finish off.

STITCH GUIDE

TREBLE CROCHET *(abbreviated tr)*
YO twice, insert hook in sc indicated, YO and pull up a loop (4 loops on hook), (YO and draw through 2 loops on hook) 3 times.

TRIPLE TREBLE CROCHET *(abbreviated tr tr)*
YO 4 times, insert hook in st indicated, YO and pull up a loop (6 loops on hook), (YO and draw through 2 loops on hook) 5 times.

Instructions continued on page 28.

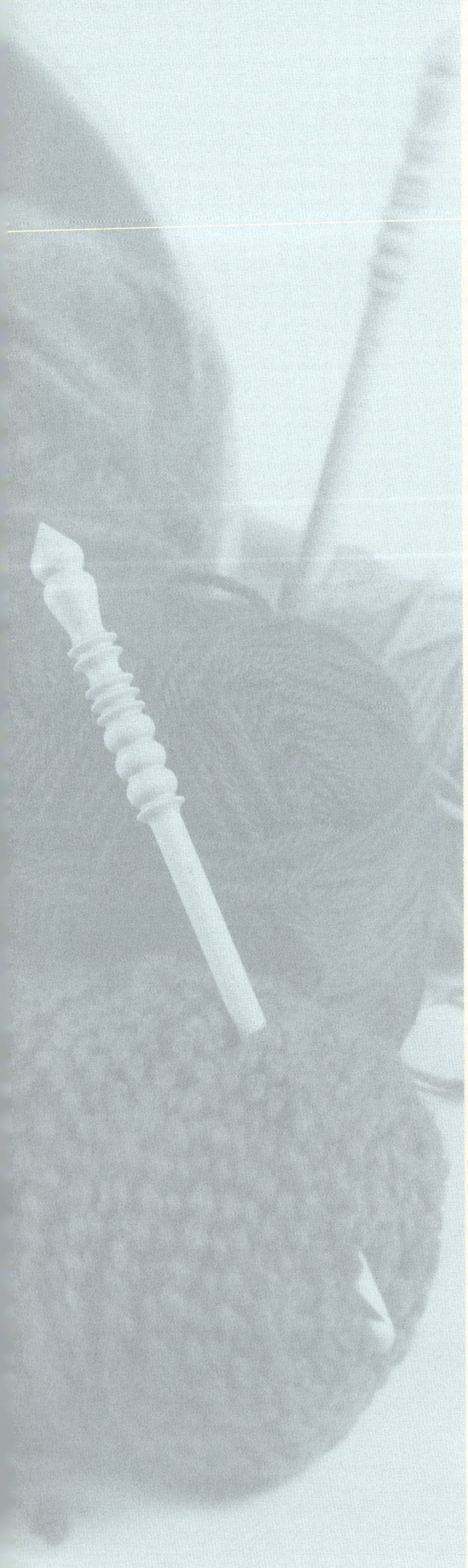

BODY

Ch 122.

Row 1: Sc in second ch from hook and in each ch across: 121 sc.

Row 2 (Right side)**:** Ch 1, turn; sc in Front Loop Only of first 3 sc ***(Fig. 1, page 35)***, skip next 2 sc, 7 dc in **both** loops of next sc, ★ skip next 2 sc, sc in Front Loop Only of next 5 sc, skip next 2 sc, 7 dc in **both** loops of next sc; repeat from ★ across to last 5 sc, skip next 2 sc, sc in Front Loop Only of last 3 sc: 12 7-dc groups.

Note: Loop a short piece of thread around any stitch to mark Row 2 as **right** side.

Row 3: Ch 1, turn; sc in Back Loop Only of first 3 sc, ch 2, skip next 3 dc, 7 dc in **both** loops of next dc, ch 2, ★ skip next 3 dc, sc in Back Loop Only of next 5 sc, ch 2, skip next 3 dc, 7 dc in **both** loops of next dc, ch 2; repeat from ★ across to last 6 sts, skip next 3 dc, sc in Back Loop Only of last 3 sc.

Row 4: Ch 5 **(counts as first tr tr)**, turn; working in both loops, tr tr in same st, ch 3, skip next ch-2 sp and next 3 dc, sc in next dc, ch 3, ★ skip next ch-2 sp and next 2 sc, 3 tr tr in next sc, ch 3, skip next ch-2 sp and next 3 dc, sc in next dc, ch 3; repeat from ★ across to last ch-2 sp, skip last ch-2 sp and next 2 sc, 2 tr tr in last sc: 49 sts and 24 ch-3 sps.

Row 5: Ch 1, turn; sc in first 2 tr tr, 3 sc in next ch-3 sp, sc in next sc, 3 sc in next ch-3 sp, ★ sc in next 3 tr tr, 3 sc in next ch-3 sp, sc in next sc, 3 sc in next ch-3 sp; repeat from ★ across to last 2 tr tr, sc in last 2 tr tr: 121 sc.

Row 6: Ch 3 **(counts as first dc, now and throughout)**, turn; 3 dc in same st, skip next 2 sc, sc in Front Loop Only of next 5 sc, ★ skip next 2 sc, 7 dc in **both** loops of next sc, skip next 2 sc, sc in Front Loop Only of next 5 sc; repeat from ★ across to last 3 sc, skip next 2 sc, 4 dc in last sc: 11 7-dc groups and 2 4-dc groups.

Row 7: Ch 3, turn; 3 dc in same st, ch 2, skip next 3 dc, sc in Back Loop Only of next 5 sc, ch 2, ★ skip next 3 dc, 7 dc in **both** loops of next dc, ch 2, skip next 3 dc, sc in Back Loop Only of next 5 sc, ch 2; repeat from ★ across to last 4 dc, skip next 3 dc, 4 dc in last dc.

Row 8: Ch 1, turn; working in both loops, sc in first dc, ★ ch 3, skip next ch-2 sp and next 2 sc, 3 tr tr in next sc, ch 3, skip next ch-2 sp and next 3 dc, sc in next dc; repeat from ★ across: 49 sts and 24 ch-3 sps.

Row 9: Ch 1, turn; sc in first sc, ★ 3 sc in next ch-3 sp, sc in next 3 tr tr, 3 sc in next ch-3 sp, sc in next sc; repeat from ★ across: 121 sc.

Row 10: Ch 1, turn; sc in Front Loop Only of first 3 sc, skip next 2 sc, 7 dc in **both** loops of next sc, ★ skip next 2 sc, sc in Front Loop Only of next 5 sc, skip next 2 sc, 7 dc in **both** loops of next sc; repeat from ★ across to last 5 sc, skip next 2 sc, sc in Front Loop Only of last 3 sc: 12 7-dc groups.

Repeat Rows 3-10 for pattern until piece measures 19" (48.5 cm) from beginning ch, ending by working Row 8; do **not** finish off.

Joining: Ch 1; with **right** side together, working in free loops of beginning ch ***(Fig. 2b, page 35)*** and in sts on last row, sc evenly across; do **not** finish off.

FIRST END EDGING

Rnd 1: Ch 3; with **wrong** side facing, work 143 dc evenly spaced around end of rows; join with slip st to first dc: 144 dc.

Rnd 2: Ch 3, turn; dc in next dc and in each dc around.

Rnd 3: Ch 1, do **not** turn; sc in same st, ★ ch 7, skip next 5 dc, sc in next dc; repeat from ★ around to last 5 dc, skip last 5 dc, ch 3, tr in first sc to form last ch-7 sp: 24 ch-7 sps.

Rnds 4-13: Ch 1, sc in last ch-7 sp made, (ch 7, sc in next ch-7 sp) around, ch 3, tr in first sc to form last ch-7 sp.

Rnd 14: Ch 1, sc in last ch-7 sp made, ch 4, (sc in next ch-7 sp, ch 4) around; join with slip st to first sc.

Rnd 15: 9 Dc in next ch-4 sp, (slip st in next sc, 9 dc in next ch-4 sp) around; join with slip st to joining slip st, finish off.

SECOND END EDGING

Rnd 1: With **wrong** side facing, join thread with dc in seam ***(see Joining With Dc, page 34)***; work 143 dc evenly spaced around end of rows; join with slip st to first dc: 144 dc.

Rnds 2-15: Work same as First End Edging.

FINISHING

Turn Body **right** side out; then insert pillow form.

Layer the ribbons and wrap them around one End Edging; then tie in a knot and trim ends.

Repeat for second end.

bachelor's buttons

I love to embroider, but am not always happy with my results when I attempt to freehand. So I used the rows of chain spaces to make sure the embroidered lines were symmetrical, and appliquéd the small motifs right onto the front.

EASY +

Finished Size:
20" (51 cm) square

MATERIALS
MEDIUM 4
Medium Weight Yarn
[4 ounces, 186 yards
(113 grams, 170 meters) per skein]:
Blue - 2 skeins
Rust, Yellow, Orange, and Brown - one skein **each** color
Crochet hook, size H (5 mm) **or** size needed for gauge
Pillow form - 20" (51 cm) square
5/8" (16 mm) Buttons - 5
Sewing needle and thread
Yarn needle

GAUGE: In pattern, 16 sc and 16 rows = 4" (10 cm)

Gauge Swatch: 4" (10 cm) square
With Blue, ch 17.
Work same as Back for 16 rows.
Finish off.

STITCH GUIDE

TREBLE CROCHET ***(abbreviated tr)***
YO twice, insert hook in sp indicated, YO and pull up a loop (4 loops on hook), (YO and draw through 2 loops on hook) 3 times.

DOUBLE TREBLE CROCHET ***(abbreviated dtr)***
YO 3 times, insert hook in sp indicated, YO and pull up a loop (5 loops on hook), (YO and draw through 2 loops on hook) 4 times.

FRONT

With Blue, ch 81.

Row 1 (Right side): Sc in second ch from hook and in each ch across: 80 sc.

Note: Loop a short piece of yarn around any stitch to mark Row 1 as **right** side.

Row 2: Ch 1, turn; sc in first sc, sc in Front Loop Only of next sc and each sc across to last sc ***(Fig. 1, page 35)***, sc in **both** loops of last sc.

Row 3: Ch 1, turn; sc in first sc, sc in Back Loop Only of next sc and each sc across to last sc, sc in **both** loops of last sc.

Rows 4-10: Repeat Rows 2 and 3, 3 times; then repeat Row 2 once **more**.

Row 11: Ch 1, turn; sc in first sc, ch 1, ★ skip next sc, sc in Back Loop Only of next sc, ch 1; repeat from ★ 21 times **more**, skip next sc, sc in Back Loop Only of each sc across to last sc, sc in **both** loops of last sc: 57 sc and 23 chs.

Row 12: Ch 1, turn; sc in first sc, sc in Front Loop Only of each sc and each ch across to last sc, sc in **both** loops of last sc: 80 sc.

Row 13: Ch 1, turn; sc in first sc, sc in Back Loop Only of next sc and each sc across to last sc, sc in **both** loops of last sc.

Rows 14-24: Repeat Rows 2 and 3, 5 times; then repeat Row 2 once **more**.

Instructions continued on page 32.

Row 25: Ch 1, turn; sc in first sc, ch 1, ★ skip next sc, sc in Back Loop Only of next sc, ch 1; repeat from ★ 24 times **more**, skip next sc, sc in Back Loop Only of each sc across to last sc, sc in **both** loops of last sc: 54 sc and 26 chs.

Rows 26-38: Repeat Rows 12-24.

Row 39: Ch 1, turn; sc in first sc, ch 1, ★ skip next sc, sc in Back Loop Only of next sc, ch 1; repeat from ★ 19 times **more**, skip next sc, sc in Back Loop Only of each sc across to last sc, sc in **both** loops of last sc: 59 sc and 21 chs.

Rows 40-52: Repeat Rows 12-24.

Row 53: Ch 1, turn; sc in first sc, ch 1, ★ skip next sc, sc in Back Loop Only of next sc, ch 1; repeat from ★ 16 times **more**, skip next sc, sc in Back Loop Only of each sc across to last sc, sc in **both** loops of last sc: 62 sc and 18 chs.

Rows 54-66: Repeat Rows 12-24.

Row 67: Ch 1, turn; sc in first sc, ch 1, ★ skip next sc, sc in Back Loop Only of next sc, ch 1; repeat from ★ 8 times **more**, skip next sc, sc in Back Loop Only of each sc across to last sc, sc in **both** loops of last sc: 70 sc and 10 chs.

Rows 68-80: Repeat Rows 12-24.

Row 81: Ch 1, turn; sc in first sc, sc in Back Loop Only of next sc and each sc across to last sc, sc in **both** loops of last sc; finish off.

FLOWER

(Make 5 - 2 each Yellow and Rust, and one Orange)

Ch 4; join with slip st to form a ring.

Rnd 1 (Right side): Ch 3 **(counts as first dc)**, (8 dc, tr, 2 dtr, tr, sc) in ring; join with slip st to first dc, finish off leaving long end for sewing.

Note: Mark Rnd 1 as **right** side.

STEM

With **right** side of Front facing and beginning ch to your left, insert hook in first st on Row 11 from **front** to **back**, holding Brown on **wrong** side, YO and pull up a loop, ★ insert hook in next ch-1 sp, YO and draw though sp and loop on hook; repeat from ★ across; finish off.

Repeat for Rows 25, 39, 53, and 67.

Thread needle with long end and using photo as a guide, sew one Flower to top of each Stem.

Sew button to center of each Flower.

BACK

With Blue, ch 81.

Row 1 (Right side): Sc in second ch from hook and in each ch across. 80 sc.

Note: Mark Row 1 as **right** side.

Row 2: Ch 1, turn; sc in first sc, sc in Front Loop Only of next sc and each sc across to last sc, sc in **both** loops of last sc.

Row 3: Ch 1, turn; sc in first sc, sc in Back Loop Only of next sc and each sc across to last sc, sc in **both** loops of last sc.

Rows 4-81: Repeat Rows 2 and 3, 39 times.

Finish off.

JOINING

With **wrong** sides and last rows of Front and Back together, Front facing, and working through **both** layers, join Blue with sc in first sc on last row ***(see Joining With Sc, page 34)***; sc evenly around working (sc, ch 1, sc) in each corner and inserting pillow form before closing; join with slip st to first sc, finish off.

generalinstructions

ABBREVIATIONS

ch(s)	chain(s)
cm	centimeters
dc	double crochet(s)
dtr	double treble crochet(s)
hdc	half double crochet(s)
MC	Main Color
mm	millimeters
Rnd(s)	Round(s)
sc	single crochet(s)
sp(s)	space(s)
st(s)	stitch(es)
tr	treble crochet(s)
tr tr	triple treble crochet(s)
YO	yarn over

★ — work instructions following ★ as many **more** times as indicated in addition to the first time.

† to † — work all instructions from first † to second † **as many** times as specified.

( ) or [ ] — work enclosed instructions **as many** times as specified by the number immediately following **or** work all enclosed instructions in the stitch or space indicated **or** contains explanatory remarks.

colon (:) — the number(s) given after a colon at the end of a row or round denote(s) the number of stitches or spaces you should have on that row or round.

CROCHET TERMINOLOGY		
UNITED STATES		INTERNATIONAL
slip stitch (slip st)	=	single crochet (sc)
single crochet (sc)	=	double crochet (dc)
half double crochet (hdc)	=	half treble crochet (htr)
double crochet (dc)	=	treble crochet(tr)
treble crochet (tr)	=	double treble crochet (dtr)
double treble crochet (dtr)	=	triple treble crochet (ttr)
triple treble crochet (tr tr)	=	quadruple treble crochet (qtr)
skip	=	miss

CROCHET HOOKS	
Metric mm	U.S.
2.25	B-1
2.75	C-2
3.25	D-3
3.5	E-4
3.75	F-5
4	G-6
5	H-8
5.5	I-9
6	J-10
6.5	K-10½
9	N
10	P
15	Q

STEEL CROCHET HOOKS	
UNITED STATES	METRIC (mm)
00	3.5
0	3.25
1	2.75
2	2.25
3	2.1
4	2
5	1.9
6	1.8
7	1.65
8	1.5
9	1.4
10	1.3
11	1.1
12	1
13	0.85
14	0.75

GAUGE

Exact gauge is **essential** for proper size. Before beginning your project, make the sample swatch given in the individual instructions in the yarn or thread and hook specified. After completing the swatch, measure it, counting your stitches and rows or rounds carefully. If your swatch is larger or smaller than specified, **make another, changing hook size to get the correct gauge.** Keep trying until you find the size hook that will give you the specified gauge.

MARKERS

Markers are used to help distinguish the beginning of each round being worked. Place a 2" (5 cm) scrap piece of yarn before the first stitch of each round, moving marker after each round is complete.

JOINING WITH SC

When instructed to join with sc, begin with a slip knot on hook. Insert hook in stitch or space indicated, YO and pull up a loop, YO and draw through both loops on hook.

JOINING WITH HDC

When instructed to join with hdc, begin with a slip knot on hook. YO, holding loop on hook, insert hook in stitch or space indicated, YO and pull up a loop (3 loops on hook), YO and draw through all 3 loops on hook.

JOINING WITH DC

When instructed to join with dc, begin with a slip knot on hook. YO, holding loop on hook, insert hook in stitch or space indicated, YO and pull up a loop (3 loops on hook), (YO and draw through 2 loops on hook) twice.

Yarn Weight Symbol & Names	LACE 0	SUPER FINE 1	FINE 2	LIGHT 3	MEDIUM 4	BULKY 5	SUPER BULKY 6
Type of Yarns in Category	Fingering, 10-count crochet thread	Sock, Fingering Baby	Sport, Baby	DK, Light Worsted	Worsted, Afghan, Aran	Chunky, Craft, Rug	Bulky, Roving
Crochet Gauge* Ranges in Single Crochet to 4" (10 cm)	32-42 double crochets**	21-32 sts	16-20 sts	12-17 sts	11-14 sts	8-11 sts	5-9 sts
Advised Hook Size Range	Steel*** 6,7,8 Regular hook B-1	B-1 to E-4	E-4 to 7	7 to I-9	I-9 to K-10.5	K-10.5 to M-13	M-13 and larger

*GUIDELINES ONLY: The chart above reflects the most commonly used gauges and hook sizes for specific yarn categories.

** Lace weight yarns are usually crocheted on larger-size hooks to create lacy openwork patterns. Accordingly, a gauge range is difficult to determine. Always follow the gauge stated in your pattern.

*** Steel crochet hooks are sized differently from regular hooks–the higher the number the smaller the hook, which is the reverse of regular hook sizing.

BEGINNER	Projects for first-time crocheters using basic stitches. Minimal shaping.
EASY	Projects using yarn with basic stitches, repetitive stitch patterns, simple color changes, and simple shaping and finishing.
INTERMEDIATE	Projects using a variety of techniques, such as basic lace patterns or color patterns, mid-level shaping and finishing.
EXPERIENCED	Projects with intricate stitch patterns, techniques and dimension, such as non-repeating patterns, multi-color techniques, fine threads, small hooks, detailed shaping and refined finishing.

BACK OR FRONT LOOP ONLY

Work only in loop(s) indicated by arrow *(Fig. 1)*.

Fig. 1

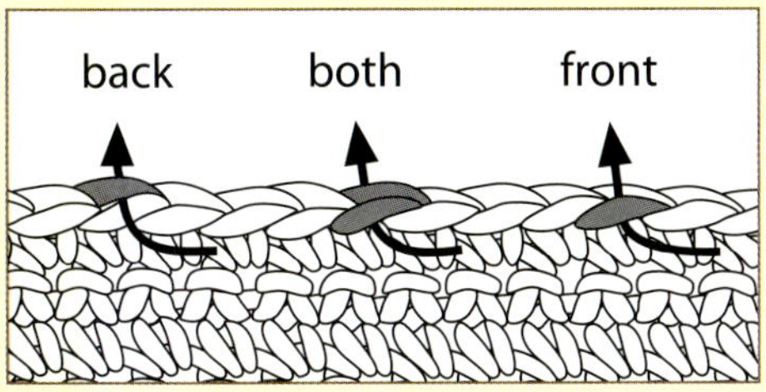

FREE LOOPS

After working in Back or Front Loops Only on a row or round, there will be a ridge of unused loops. These are called the free loops. Later, when instructed to work in the free loops of the same row or round, work in these loops ***(Fig. 2a)***. When instructed to work in free loops of a chain, work in loop indicated by arrow ***(Fig. 2b)***.

Fig. 2a

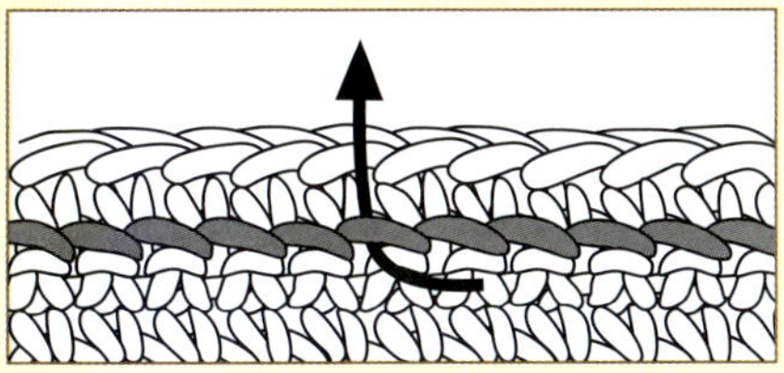

Fig. 2b

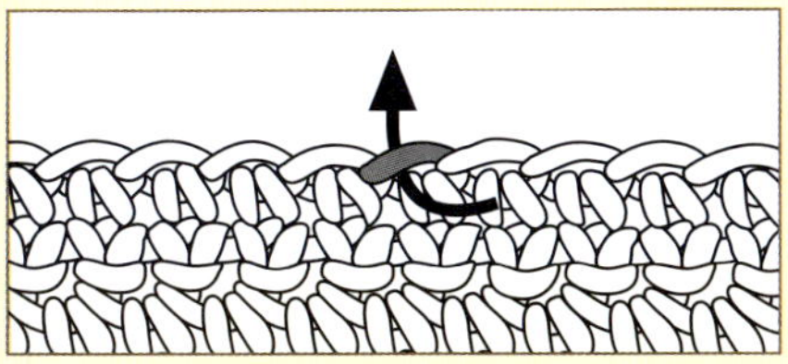

CHANGING COLORS

Work the last stitch to within one step of completion, hook new yarn ***(Fig. 3a or Fig. 3b)*** and draw through all loops on hook.

Fig. 3a

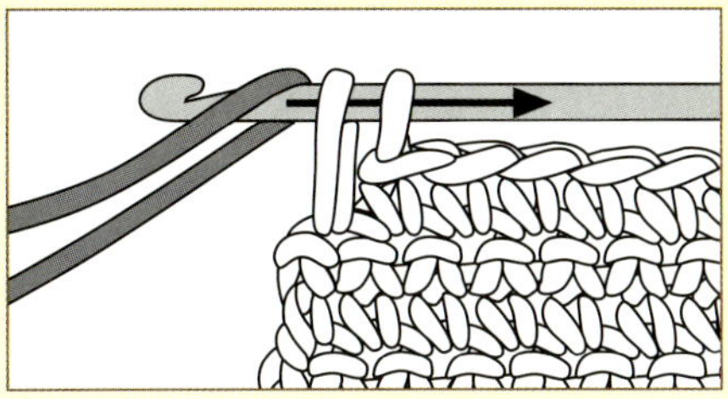

Fig. 3b

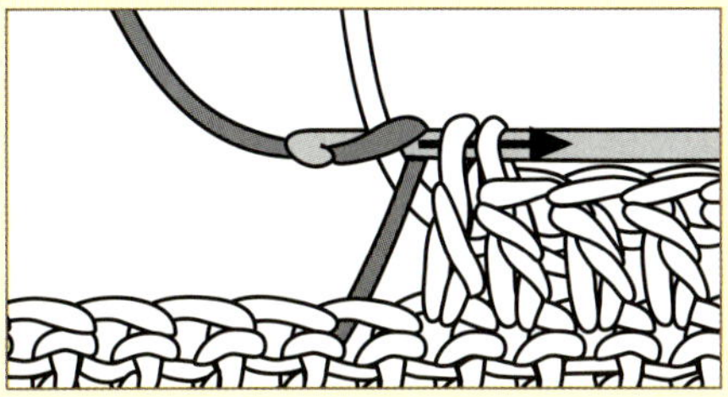

REVERSE SINGLE CROCHET

(abbreviated reverse sc)

Working from **left** to **right**, ★ insert hook in st to right of hook ***(Fig. 4a)***, YO and draw through, under and to left of loop on hook (2 loops on hook) ***(Fig. 4b)***, YO and draw through both loops on hook ***(Fig. 4c)* (reverse sc made, *Fig. 4d*)**; repeat from ★ around.

Fig. 4a

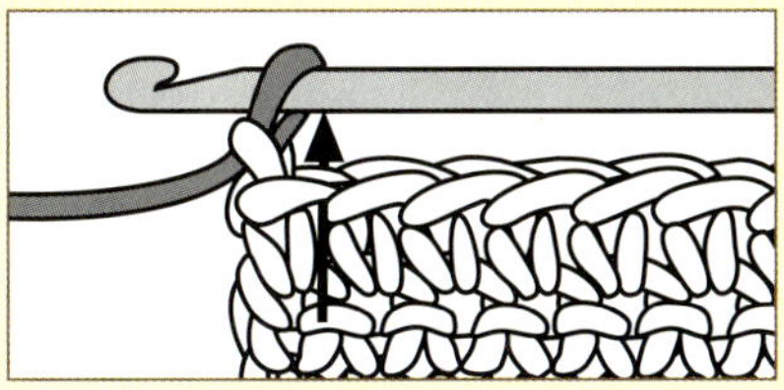

Fig. 4b

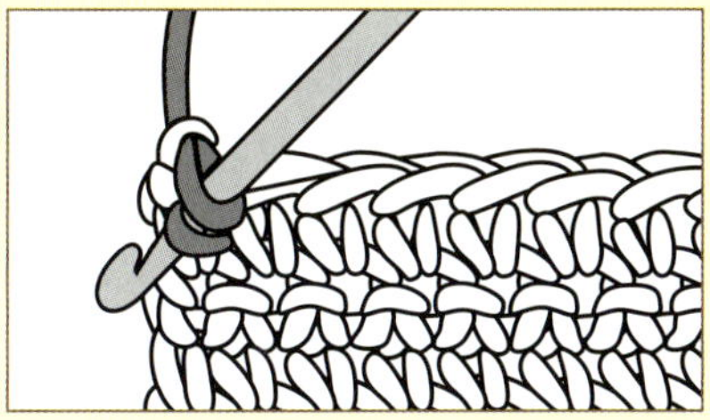

Fig. 4c

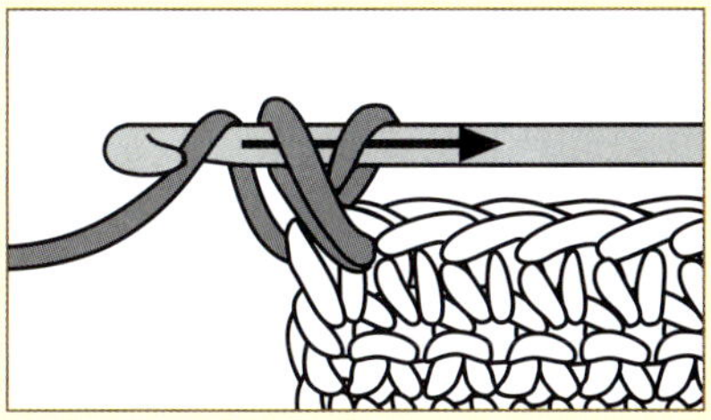

Fig. 4d

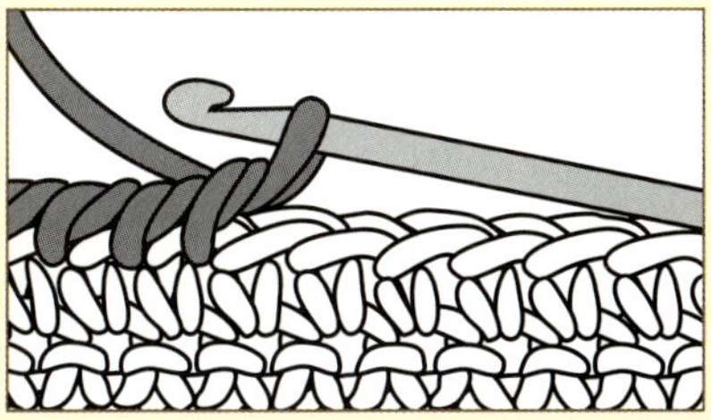

We would like to thank Soft Touch for providing Home Faux Down pillow forms for our photo models.

YARN INFORMATION

Each Pillow in this leaflet was made with Light Weight or Medium Weight Yarn with the exception of A Little Luxury which was made using bedspread weight cotton thread (size 10). Any brand of Light Weight or Medium Weight Yarn may be used. It is best to refer to the yardage/meters when determining how many balls or skeins to purchase. Remember, to arrive at the finished size, it is the GAUGE/TENSION that is important, not the brand of yarn.

For your convenience, listed below are colors used to create our photography models.

LOOP-DE-LOOP
LB Collection® Cotton Bamboo
Blue - #107 Hyacinth
Ecru - #098 Magnolia
Green - #174 Snapdragon

FRESH IDEA
Red Heart® Eco-Ways™
Green - #3523 Asparagus
Lt Green - #1615 Lichen

ART DECO
Lion Brand® Microspun
Brown - #126 Coffee
Green - #134 Leaf
Orange - #186 Mango

BUTTONED UP
Red Heart® Eco-Ways™
Green - #3523 Asparagus
Ecru - #3334 Sand

ALFRESCO
Premier™ Yarns Dream
MC (Blue) - #24-223 Carolina Sky
Green - #24-216 Baby Fern
Teal - #24-219 Tucson Teal
Lt Blue - #24-221 Baby Blue
Dk Blue - #24-225 Navy
Purple - #24-227 Heather

HAPPY PATCHES
Red Heart® Soft Yarn®
Blue - #2515 Turquoise
Black - #4614 Black
Rose - #9779 Berry

TEMPTING TEXTURE
Patons® Canadiana
Blue - #10134 Royal Blue
Lion Brand® Glitterspun®
Silver - #150 Silver

ALL-A-WHIRL
Naturally Caron® Country
#0017 Claret

A LITTLE LUXURY
DMC® Cebelia (size 10)
Blanc

BACHELOR'S BUTTONS
Red Heart® Eco-Ways™
Blue - #1821 Blue Cloud
Rust - #3275 Cinnabar
Yellow - #3114 Chamois
Brown - #3360 Mushroom
Orange - #3422 Yam

We have made every effort to ensure that these instructions are accurate and complete. We cannot, however, be responsible for human error, typographical mistakes, or variations in individual work.

Production Team: Instructional Editor - Lois J. Long; Technical Editor - Sarah J. Green; Editorial Writer - Susan McManus Johnson; Senior Graphic Artist - Lora Puls; Graphic Artists - Jacob Casleton, Becca Snider and Janie Marie Wright; Photo Stylist - Sondra Daniel; and Photographer - Ken West.

Instructions tested and photo models made by Marianna Crowder.